# NUMEROLOGY

ANCIENT WISDOM FOR THE NEW AGE

# NUMEROLOGY

THE SECRETS OF NUMBERS

Dr. Greg Russell

IMM lifestyle books
Read. Learn. Do What You Love.

Text, illustrations, and photographs by IMM Lifestyle Books, an imprint of Fox Chapel Publishing, 903 Square Street, Mount Joy, PA 17552. *www.foxchapelpublishing.com*

First published in 1998 by New Holland (Publishers) Ltd



Designed and edited by
Complete Editions
40 Castelnau
London SW13 9RU

Editorial Direction: Yvonne McFarlane
Editor: Michèle Brown
Designer: Peter Ward

ISBN 978-1-5048-0159-1

Printed in China
First Printing

FSC www.fsc.org MIX Paper | Supporting responsible forestry FSC® C147414

To learn more about the other great books from Fox Chapel Publishing, or to find a retail near you, call toll-free at 800-457-9112 or visit us at *www.FoxChapelPublishing.com.*

We are always looking for talented authors. To submit an idea, please send a brief inquiry to acquisitions@foxchapelpublishing.com.

Or write to:
Fox Chapel Publishing
903 Square Street
Mount Joy, PA 17552

# CONTENTS

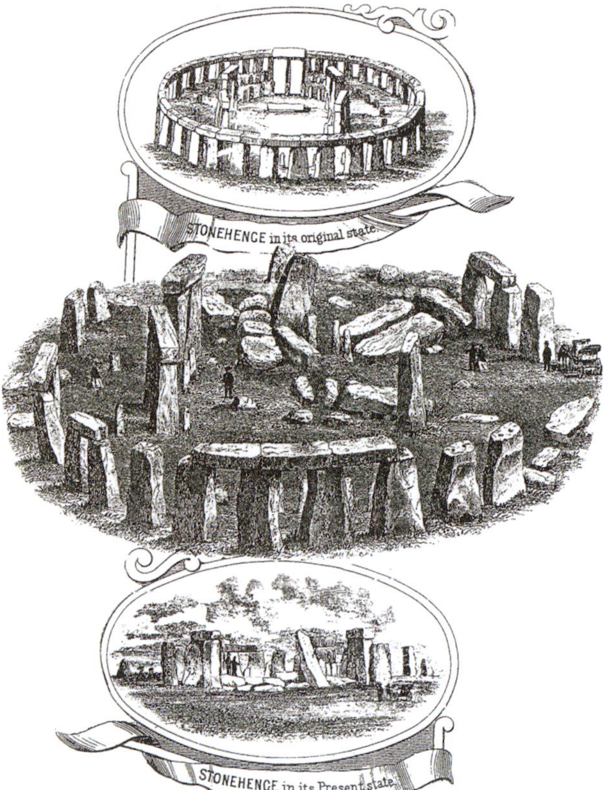
STONEHENCE in its original state.
STONEHENCE in its Present state.

# ACROSS THE MILLENIA

Was Stonehenge the first computer? Did the dimensions of the Great Pyramids conceal universal truths? The deep meaning contained by numbers has fascinated people for thousands of years, though much of the early recorded history is lost. Fragments of carvings and manuscripts from Egypt, China and India give an insight into the minds of the early mathematicians. Claims are made that numerology was being studied 10,000 years ago by the Babylonians and Egyptians, but this must be speculation.

It is commonly thought that the Arabs devised numbers as we know them, but it is claimed in the ancient Hindu writings, the *Vedas* and *Upanashads*, that they acquired the basic knowledge from

the Hindus. They in turn claim to have acquired them from the Gods.

The Chinese, influenced by the widely travelled Phoenicians, ascribed the qualities of heat, fire, sun, daytime and the colour white to the odd numbers. The even numbers were ascribed cold, water, moon, darkness and the colour black. These attributes were absorbed by the father of mathematics and numerology, Pythagoras, into his system in the sixth century bc. He believed that the movement of the planets, the ever-changing seasons and all actions of the human race could be codified into mathematical laws. At his school at Croton, in Italy, the Greek philosopher propounded many of the basic tenets of both mathematics and numerology which remain the same today. He believed that everything could be reduced to mathematical terms and postulated the theory

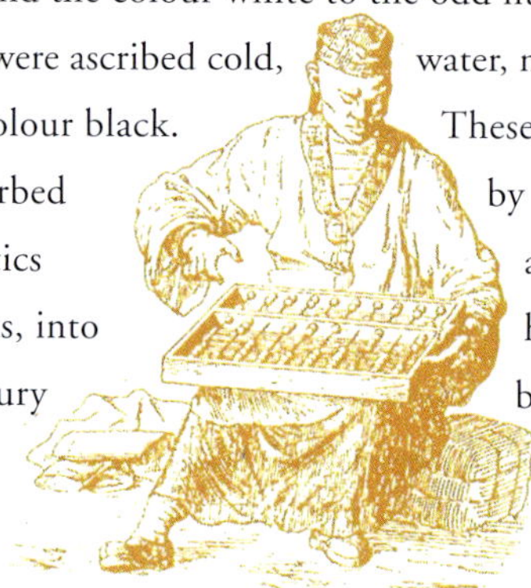

"RAPHAEL'S WITCH" OR "ORACLE OF THE FUTURE."
THE DESTRUCTION OF POMPEII.
RAPHAEL'S VISION.
THE ENCHANTRESS OF THE WATERS.
THE MYSTICAL WHEEL OF PYTHAGORAS
THE FIRST FIVE COLOURED DESIGNS BY RAPHAEL & R. CRUIKSHANK.

of opposition. The basic opposition of odd and even is followed by limited and unlimited, one and many, right and left, male and female, rest and motion, straight and curved, light and darkness, good and evil, square and oblong.

The Hebrews had a different system, which continued the tradition of translating letters into numbers. Contained in the mysteries of the *Kabbalah*, much of its meaning has been lost in the mists of time. Their system, known as Gemetria, employs the 22 letters of the Hebrew alphabet, each having several layers of meaning, often gleaned from their appearance in the books of the Old Testament.

During the Renaissance, a numerological sytem was devised by Henry Agrippa, and in the 18th century it was elaborated by Count Cagliostro. Both of these systems were heavily mystical and related to the *Kabbalah*. It is from this time that the use of a reduction of a person's name into numbers came into use.

Voltaire was interested in numerology and wrote that "There is no such thing as chance. We have created this word to express the known effect of an unknown cause."

In the early 20th century the principal practitioner was Count Louis Hamon, who practised numerology under the name of Cheiro. He also single-handedly created modern palmistry. His clients included the world's nobility and his textbooks are still the standard works of reference on both subjects.

The use of numbers crosses barriers of language, class and race, reflecting their universality. To reduce the human personality to numbers may appear cold and calculating, ignoring the mystical and spiritual elements. But the numbers themselves are representatives of the myriad elements which make up our universe, from the tiniest particle within an atom to the wider mystery of the cosmos. As the new millenium approaches, we can learn from the previous ones and illuminate our lives by the power of numbers.

# HEAVENLY NUMBERS

There is a symbiotic connection between numbers and astrology which has been known for centuries. Our universe has been reduced to numbers by ancient mathematicians and modern atomic theorists. Each astrological sign is assigned a planet and a corresponding number which can be assumed to have corresponding attributes.

| Star Sign | Ruler | Number |
|---|---|---|
| Aries | Mars | 9 |
| Taurus | Venus | 6 |
| Gemini | Mercury | 5 |
| Cancer | Moon | 2 and 7 |
| Leo | Sun | 1 and 4 |
| Virgo | Mercury | 5 |
| Libra | Venus | 6 |
| Scorpio | Mars | 9 |
| Sagittarius | Jupiter | 3 |
| Capricorn | Saturn | 8 |
| Aquarius | Saturn | 8 |
| Pisces | Jupiter | 3 |

The Sun and Moon are allocated two numbers for historical reasons, as there were only seven planets when much of the serious formulation of astrology took place. Uranus has been allotted four, Neptune seven and Pluto both eight and nine. These influences remain slight, but when consulting an astrological text it does no harm to consider their position.

# FROM NOTHINGNESS

Numerology concerns itself with the numbers one to nine, to which all other numbers reduce, such as the birth number, the name number, the vowel number and the consonant number. Nothing, nought or zero (0) cannot enter the calculation as it adds nothing at the beginning of the sequence and adds nothing to any other digit it may accompany, such as ten (10) or one hundred (100). It can, however, be given a place in the scheme of things as the number, or lack of number, which epitomizes the void, the nothingness out of which all creation emerged. It can be used to symbolise the universe as we see it, in the case of Brahmin as the universal egg. It can mean the infinitely great or the infinitely small. It can be the universe or the atomic particle.

The number ten exists only as a composite of number one, the Sun number, expressed as 10 = 1+0 = 1. It is the first such composite number, of which all have to be reduced to a single digit for their meaning to be realized.

# BIRTH, MIND AND DESTINY NUMBERS

These numbers are derived from the birth date, expressed as the numbers of the day, month and years. The day number lies between 1 and 31, the month between 1 and 12, starting with January, followed by the year. American usage reverses the day and the month, so take this into account when calculating the mind and destiny numbers.

The day or mind number will either be from 1 to 9, or the total of the digits of the day. If born on the 19th, the mind number would be reduced as 1+9=10 and then 1+0=1. This number shows how you see yourself.

The destiny number is the single whole number reduced from the total birth date. Add all the numbers together and reduce to a single digit. For example, if your birth date was the 2nd of June 1960, this number would be:

$2 + 6 + 1 + 9 + 6 + 0 = 24$

$2 + 4 = 6$

Thus 6, the number of sexual attraction, ruled by the goddess Venus, and the colour green, as depicted by verdant and prolific plant life, is the birth number (*see page* 28). This conveys what you deserve or expect.

Other significant numbers, explained later, include the Name Number, revealing formation of character, the Vowel Number, representing the ego and outward appearance, and the Consonant Number, revealing the id, the inner self.

# 1

This number is associated with the sun and astrological fire signs, Leo, Sagittarius and Aries. They all spell leadership, symbolized by the Ancient Egyptians as Khepri, the rising sun heralding a new day. It is the number of the resurrected in many religions, such as Jesus Christ or Osiris. Being the first number, rising from nothing or chaos, it is that of new beginnings, of breaks with the past

and of boundless energy. It is usually described as being masculine and assertive.

If born on the 1st of any month, or even, more importantly, the 11th, this number will feature heavily in life. If it is the birth number, it is likely that the physique will be lean and athletic, with striking looks to match. A leonine mane of hair, often blond, is a feature. One is the number of gold and it is likely that perfect skin will tan easily in the sun's rays. The total effect is of action and vibrancy, fitness and good health.

One is also the first, young number, so there can be an immature streak, a hint of the young child in the personality. Trying to lead people who do not wish to be led can mean a tendency to sulk or bear grudges. And as you see yourself as a leader, you rarely wish to be led. Needing loyalty can lead to feelings of being slighted at the smallest offence.

Being acclaimed number one by all does not mean that you can always assume you are number one. Beware vanity!

## 2

This number is linked to the Moon, being second in importance to the Sun in most mythologies. The two points of the arc of the new Moon are linked to twins, such as Castor and Pollux, known as Gemini in astrology. But they are also associated with the two horns of the Devil as well as his cloven hooves. Over the centuries, the Moon evolved from being a male planet to a symbol of femininity, as its cycle corresponds to the menstrual cycle. It is also regarded as graceful, cool and mystical, essentially feminine attributes.

Those born on the 2nd, or the 20th or 22nd, have strong traits related to the Moon's mythical past, together with strong intuition, deep powers of thought and notable sensitivity. Men born on these dates can show feminine attributes, a slight physique, a tendency to underestimate oneself and difficulties in standing one's ground. Two's colour is white and other pale watery shades, which suggests fair

skin which does not like sunlight, pale blonde hair which lacks vibrancy, and a soft voice which is rarely used to make a forceful point or to defend oneself. Beware any urge to talk with a forked tongue as this could harm a promising relationship. Remember, two's company.

# 3

This number has mystical qualities which arise from many cultures. Folk-tales have many threes, be they sisters, truths, wishes or questions. It appears in the Christian religion as the Holy Trinity of Father, Son and Holy Ghost. Lao Tze, the Chinese sage, considered that three was the number from which myriad creatures were created, creatures that embraced the yin and yang forces which are the basis of much Chinese thought. It may be that three was significant because in the countries where civilization began there were three seasons, spring (growth), summer (fruitfulness) and winter (sleep). In Greek mythology, the earth goddess Rhea gave birth to three sons, Hades, Poseidon and Zeus, who ruled the underworld, the waters and the sky. And there are the Three Graces.

Those born on the 3rd or the 30th of any month will show strong attributes of the number. These include great intelligence and wisdom, a love of life and a strong sexual appetites. The urge to reproduce is great. The physique will be solid, but can go to fat if enough care is not taken. The personality is totally outgoing, to the point that being alone is not favoured. The mind could border on the psychic and is keen on acquiring knowledge.

The colour of number three is purple which, though imperial, can also mar the complexion, warning of being too extrovert, too fond of food and drink. *Chacun à son goût.* Or, more likely, gout.

# 4

The Sun is awarded two numbers, the second being four, as its daily and yearly cycles are divided into two. This is the number of the waning Sun, whose symbol in many cultures is the serpent. The Greeks believed that the Sun God's chariot was drawn by four horses and that Zeus fathered Olympian deities, Hermes, Apollo, Artemis and Dionysus. These antecedents often favour number fours with a Greek nose. And then there are the four seasons, the four elements, the four winds, the four cardinal points and the four letters, YHVH, which represent the secret name of God in the *Kabbalah* and other mysteries.

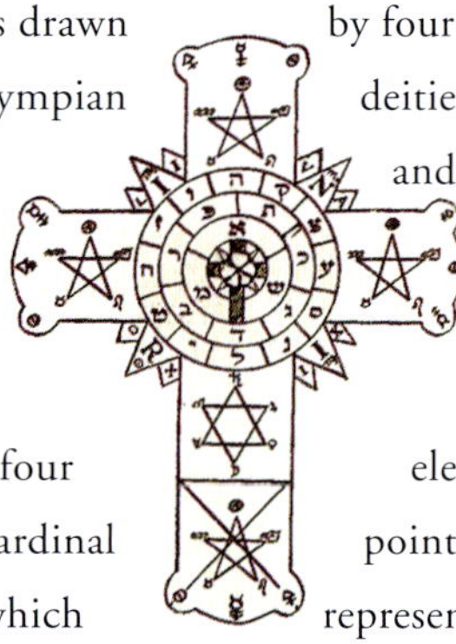

Those born on the 4th and, more importantly, the 14th, which is made up of both Sun numbers, will be of very well-balanced nature on the outside, masking a tough aggressive inside. A naturally tough body and mind is always engaged on some hard task. Work is a pleasure and its rewards are thoroughly enjoyed. Diffidence makes starting relationships difficult, not helped by a wavering lack of confidence, but once made they are firm and faithful. Think twice before unleashing that interior aggression. Remember the Four Horsemen of the Apocalypse.

# 5

This is the number of the planet Mercury, named after the Messenger of the Gods, who also conveyed the dead to the banks of the river Styx for the ferryman, Charon, to take them to the underworld. Mercury's mother was Maia, one of the Pleiades, nymphs who were pursued by Orion for five years before being transformed into stars. May, the fifth month, is named after her. The five fingers are linked to Mercury, the little finger being named after him. In early astrology there were only five planets, together with the Sun and Moon, and the Chinese saw the number five as affecting all aspects of life.

Mercury, the messenger, was constantly on the move, both physically and mentally, and these attributes are brought in both good and bad measure to those born on the 5th. Those born on the 15th are better balanced. They are likely to be of slender build, even wanting to put on weight, made impossible by their high metabolic rate and over-active behaviour. Mercury's colour is yellow, which can be reflected in the complexion, the whites of the eyes or the teeth. A way with words is another Mercury gift, with an especially silvery tongue when it comes to inveigling sexual favours. For five is the number of sexual pleasure. Many of five's good points are often cancelled by opposing bad points. Cheerful extrovert qualities can be balanced by anxiety and impatience; getting things done efficiently may be marred by endless prevaricaton. This is the mind of an innovative inventor, an avant-garde writer or an *enfant terrible* of the arts. And remember, genius is but the other side of madness.

# 6

This number has an immediate attraction as it is the symbol of love, marriage and partnership. Its planet is Venus, the goddess of love, but there is a dark side. Six is the solar number of the Sun, which reminds that love can bring pain as well as pleasure. It is the number of female sexuality and procreation. With its basis in hearth and home it also represents happiness earned through hard work. It appears in mythology as the number of children borne by the earth goddess Rhea, and the first Olympian family consisted of six gods and six goddesses. The sixth month, June, is named after Juno, the Roman goddess of marriage. In the Christian Bible, God created the world and all that is in it in six days.

Those born on the 6th, 16th or 26th, particularly if in June, can look forward to extremely fruitful relationships. There is a tendency to add weight to a good figure, unless care is taken with diet and exercise. Green is the colour of six, often reflected in large, bright eyes. A pleasing manner combines an outgoing friendliness with a degree of introversion. Friends tend to be of the quiet type, possibly with an artistic bent, reflecting six's interests. Life revolves around the home. A need to be attractive in order to make partnerships can lead to over-indulgence in clothes or cosmetics. Remember, looks aren't everything.

# 7

This is the most interesting and magical of the nine single numbers. In myths, seven is associated with sleep, peace and death. God created the world in six days, resting on the seventh, and in the ancient Babylonian *Epic of Gilgamesh*, after six days of flood and tempest the hero related how the sea grew calm on the seventh day. This is the number of the waning moon, which can presage sickness, and even death. It is also the number of occult knowledge and the unconscious mind.

Our universe is full of sevens (heptads). Seven days of the week, colours of the rainbow, pillars of wisdom, levels of the Babylonian ziggurat and branches of the Jewish menorah. For the Chinese, it governs female life, being associated with the Moon cycle. It represents time in general, through its association with Chronos, the Greek god of time, who was the seventh son of Uranus.

Those born on the 7th and the 17th can expect strong seven influences. But those born on the 27th have both lunar numbers, making even stronger Moon traits, with moods flowing constantly in cycles. July, the seventh month, was named after Julius Caesar, whose death was marked by a comet which shone for seven days. Physically, sevens are of short to medium stature, with a tendency to weight and skin problems. Smart clothes and general appearance are of no interest. However, the inner self could not be more amenable, friendly and genial reflecting seven's colour, azure blue. Weaknesses include a tendency to over-indulge. Beware the Seven Deadly Sins.

# 8

Balance and harmony are the keynote features of this number which, when horizontal, is the symbol of infinity. Its planet is Saturn, which makes it the number of dark secret places, the world of the imagination and the unconscious. It also symbolises old age, related to the old Moon, and the wisdom and patience associated with that phase of life. Sadly, it can also represent regret and disillusion, failing health and other difficulties which attend these years.

Those born on the 8th and 18th will exhibit Moon traits, but not as powerfully as those born on the 28th, which contains both lunar numbers. On the latter date, life's ups and downs will follow the phases of the Moon, and old myths about unusual behaviour at Full Moon will be found to contain a grain of truth.

If eight looms large in a birth date, there is a reasonable chance that the physique will be lanky. The teeth can be large and protruding, which hardly matters as the Saturnine character rarely smiles. There can be a certain coldness of personality, with introspection and cool emotions. This number's colour is black, or the darkest shade of other colours, which is reflected in complexion and hair. Close relations are made difficult by this coldness, the result of early maturity leading to an over-frankness when expressing opinions. Strong ideals rule the head and the heart, which can make others seek advice. Be frank, but understanding. Saturn castrated his father, Uranus. Don't cut off relations by being highly principled.

# 9

The last single odd number corresponds to the rising Sun and the fiery planet Mars, ruler of warlike activity. It is the number of rekindling the life spark, as the human gestation period is nine months. It is followed by ten which reduces to one (10=1+0=1) and thus restarts the sequence. In Greek myth, Phyllis was turned into an almond tree on the ninth night of waiting for her lover. Hephaistos, who brought fire from heaven, was reunited with his mother, Hera, in his ninth year. The nine-year-old monster twins, Otus and Ephialtes, nine fathoms tall and nine cubits wide, attempted to scale Mount Olympus by piling Mount Pelion on Mount Ossa. Every nine years, the Athenians sent their tribute of seven youths and seven maidens to Crete as an offering to the Minotaur. It is the number of wisdom and ignorance, and virtue and profligacy.

If born on the 9th, nine will be an important

influence, but not if you were born on the 19th or 29th, even if in September. This was originally the seventh month, which reduces its influence. If nine features heavily in your birth date it is likely there will be a powerful physique leading to some clumsiness. Facial hair will mar the features (a problem for women) as well as there being a higher than usual chance of a birthmark. As nine is the colour of red, it is likely that there will be a ruddy complexion and dark hair. Such minor irritations are balanced by a confident personality, which can tend to impetuosity. Mars was warlike, but often defeated through rash actions.

# WHAT'S IN A NAME

The name can be reduced to three significant numbers, the name number, the vowel number and the consonant number, all of which have particular attributes. All three are calculated using the number equivalents of the letters of the alphabet as shown:

| 1 | 2 | 3 | 4 | 5 | 6 | 7 | 8 | 9 |
|---|---|---|---|---|---|---|---|---|
| A | B | C | D | E | F | G | H | I |
| J | K | L | M | N | O | P | Q | R |
| S | T | U | V | W | X | Y | Z | |

To calculate the name number take the letter values and reduce them to a single digit as demonstrated;

P E T E R P A N

7 + 5 + 2 + 5 + 9 7 + 1 + 5 = 41

4 + 1 = 5

Five is related to Mercury, the messenger, and suggests a slender build and sexual ambivalence. This description fits Peter Pan perfectly, even though he is fictional.

Name numbers represent inherent character, which can change over the years. It is possible that someone christened and called Robert during childhood may abbreviate the name to the more casual Bob as a teenager. And so the name number will change, reflecting the developing character. Similarly, on marriage a woman may take her husband's surname, possibly changing her name number. This can reflect the nature of the marriage.

## *The Name Vowel Number*

The vowel number represents the Freudian ego, the exposed and conscious outer self. The consonant number, which follows, represents the id, the inner character.

The vowel number is calculated by taking the vowel numbers from the preceding chart and reducing them to a single digit;

| P | E | T | E | R | P | A | N | |
|---|---|---|---|---|---|---|---|---|
| | 5 | | + 5 | | | + 1 | | = 11 |
| | | | | | | 1 + 1 | | = 2 |

And so Peter Pan has the strong feminine influence and fanciful qualities associated with the Moon.

Vowel propensities in brief are:

**One:** An open and confident personality, but you can believe too much in your own superiority. If not checked this can lead to selfishness, as you only give your friendship to those you regard as acolytes. Money is important for your self image. Gregariousness is a hallmark and you win friends easily. The best balancing id number is five, the setting sun.

**Two:** While lacking self-confidence and being very laid back, you harbour great creative talents. You use your own hesitancy and diffidence to good effect. You could be a good counsellor or healer. You are best partnered by an id number of four, six or eight, as multiples of yourself will offer added support.

**Three:** Extrovert and confident, you may overindulge in the good things of life – to your detriment. Frankness and honesty may be pushed to the limit. A natural teacher, you also love to learn, especially in the fields of the arts. You also like to play the field in relationships, being matched best by a number seven id.

**Four:** Responsible, dependable and stable you may seem, but there are certain self-doubts. You are ambivalent about wanting freedom in relationships or work, but secretly hoping for a structured life. Practicality can be translated into art, as an architect or designer. You keep yourself to yourself to the point of putting off steady relationships as long as possible. You are best partnered by an eight id, as they can put up with you and your moods.

**Five:** A clever mind which can cope with anything new, but it makes you short-fused. Intellectual games are preferred, as well as learning languages or new skills. Close commitments are kept at arm's length as they interfere with your cerebral machinations. There is a tendency to obsession, such as cleanliness or punctuality. Your love of chatter, idle or intellectual, makes you an unreliable confidant. You are best matched by an id of one or nine, the rising Sun to balance your Sun, which is on the edge of setting. A mark of instability.

**Six:** A good, well-balanced ego, if a little reserved and over-polite. Controversy and untidiness upset, as does injustice. You can be a fence-sitter who inwardly wants to take a strong line, but is always too happy to see both sides of an argument. Relationships can be messy, especially when waning, through similar indecision. You are best matched by any even numbered id, except six.

**Seven:** Creative and bright as a button like Mercury, you tend to bounce off in all directions and don't

persevere with projects. Intellect rules, but is equally erratic. You want to please everyone. You need a strong partner to give you a helping hand, such as a number three id, that of the Sun at noon and the god Jupiter.

**Eight:** A stable and cautious number, though there may be the occasional flight of fancy. Though you are conventional, you do not much care about your appearance. You don't like sudden change and do not get on with those who are always on the move. You work slowly, but surely, to success, but when you succeed you need another goal. You are well matched by a number two id, which can reduce some of your depressive tendencies.

**Nine:** No holds are barred. You are excitable and don't mind a fight. There is no grey in this personality, things are seen only in black and white. Needing to deal with everything immediately can lead to hasty and faulty decisions. Enthusiasm and generosity can be marred by selfishness and arrogance. This rising Sun needs to be balanced by a number five id, the setting Sun.

I.U.P.I.T.E.R.

## *The Name Consonant Number*

The consonant number represents the hidden or unconscious self, the Freudian id. Ideally it should balance the ego number which has already been explained.

This number is reached by adding the number values of the letters (see the table on page 36) and reducing them to achieve a single digit.

| P | E | T | E | R | P | A | N |
|---|---|---|---|---|---|---|---|
| 7 | | + 2 | | + 9 | + 7 | | + 5 = 30 |
| | | | | | | | 3 + 0 = 3 |

Not a good match for his ego number two, as it heightens the feeling of being different, from another world, adding more fragile layers to Peter Pan's many mercurial qualities.

Consonant propensities include:

**One:** A strong sense of one's own worth and the rightness of one's own ideas. This id is a hard taskmaster and does not suffer fools gladly. A sunny personality, the ideal balance for a darker ego.

**Two:** Prolific imagination is a hallmark, to the point of living in a make-believe world. Combined with a number two ego, fantasy reigns. A more basic number is required.

**Three:** You feel different, apart from your fellows, through deep religious or psychic beliefs. But this does not stop you being an intensely sensual, if not erotic, person. Prophetic dreams lead to risk-taking, with gambling a problem. You need a very positive ego number for balance.

**Four:** Creativity is a hallmark, bound to common sense. Persistence in work can be mistaken for stubbornness as you go charging on with your myriad ideas. A rare example of the same ego and id numbers matching well.

**Five:** The number of the setting Sun can cause restlessness, making you behave in an eccentric manner at times. Stimulating though this can be, leading to travel and adventure, it is difficult to find the right ego partner. This id is secretive, so needs a sunny ego for balance.

**Six:** A philosophical demeanour, a liking for meditation and mystical learning marks this deeply private id. Playing safe, not liking change, it needs an opposite ego number to avoid total introspection and depression.

**Seven:** Another Sun number which can be a balance for some of the gloomier egos. Instinctively you know how things are and will be. You like your own company, but when alone can be prone to mild addictions like gambling, which in turn can lead to flights of unrealizable fancy.

**Eight:** Caution is a trait as this id is constantly telling you not to take risks. You don't like waste of material things or talent. But being so cautious can create an over-active sex drive through repression, which can result in great passion or great tragedy. This id needs the balance of the afternoon Sun, perhaps a four ego, to prevent going over the top.

**Nine:** Another number of deep desires, with the problem of expressing them. Coming last of the sequence, endings are a source of aggravation, a feeling of not having achieved what was hoped for. A match with a one or nine ego would be disastrous. Balance is needed.

# NUMBERS AND HEALTH

Numbers can give very general warnings about health. The destiny number, derived from the birth date, is the main influence, tempered by the three name numbers.

Whilst numbers can be a guide, the best action is for them to guide you to professional medical advice.

**One:** Liable to heart and circulation problems, suggesting care with diet and physical exertion.

**Two:** Digestive problems, partially brought on by a highly strung disposition.

**Three:** Prone to overwork, there can be nervous problems, bringing with them associated skin conditions.

**Four:** Many vegetarians possess this number, having turned to that diet to assuage nervous and digestive problems.

**Five:** Meditation is suggested to relieve insomnia, the result of overwork and constant worrying.

**Six:** The area of the throat and thorax causes troubles, but a healthy outdoor lifestyle helps alleviate them.

**Seven:** Another worrier, even when on top of things, which means that when there is aggravation, skin complaints erupt.

**Eight:** Liver problems and diseases of the blood, with occasional rheumatism, suggest a vegetarian regime to cleanse the system.

**Nine:** Children are prone to measles and fevers. Adults tend to indulge in a rich diet which can lead to a host of problems.

The only compound numbers with significance are those of the double Sun and double Moon.

**Eleven:** Plagued by nerves, over-indulgence in good things is used as a palliative, but in fact this makes things worse.

**Twenty-two:** Depressive tendencies can lead to weaknesses which bring on a whole range of illnesses.

# BIBLICAL NUMBERS

Numbers feature greatly in the Christian Bible, some having liturgical significance, others acquiring meaning by their context and relationship to numbers in other mythical texts, such as the Torah and the Kabbalah. In these texts, names have been changed not for linguistic reasons, but to alter their numerological value. The addition of an "h", making Sara become Sarah from Old to New Testaments, brings the Hebrew "Heh" into the meaning, thus adding the qualities of the number nine, suggesting spiritual fulfilment. In brief, as we traverse the Testaments, the numbers are thought to have the following interpretaions.

In the Old Testament, nothing or zero refers to the world being brought into existence, a new start, by the One God. **One** itself stands for that God, and beginning. **Two** represents opposites, day and night, man and woman,

heaven and earth, good and evil. **Three** is the first trinity, that of Adam, Eve and the first child, marking realization of three states of mind, subconscious, conscious and superconscious. **Four** is the eternal cycle of seasons which governs our lives, the four elements which surround us and the four principles of mind, body, spirit and soul of which we are made. **Five** represents the flowing senses, a river which runs through our lives and which makes us human. The five senses, when properly employed, see us through adversity, just as David took five smooth stones with which to defeat Goliath. **Six** represents the days of creation, and looks after all matters to do with home, family and all relationships. **Seven** is the most important number in the Bible, as it is the Day of the Lord. It represents the power of faith. Joshua and his priests blew trumpets around Jericho seven times and the city fell. **Eight** is the spiral of continual motion. Circumcision, achieving manhood, was carried out on the eighth day. **Nine** is achievement, the completion of the cycle.

In the New Testament, the significant numbers reach 13 as they refer to the 12 disciples and Christ himself. The first nine numbers have much the same attributes as those in the Old Testament, with three achieving greater meaning as the Second Trinity, the Father, Son and Holy Ghost. Its relationship to the mind is strengthened by Jesus asking Peter "Dost thou love me" three times, appealing to all levels of consciousness. Jesus also rose three times, was denied three times by Peter and was the third person crucified at Golgotha. Judas received 30 pieces of silver and the 12 disciples resonate three in two different ways, 12÷4=3 and 1+2=3. **Ten**, as we have seen earlier, is a composite number and as such takes on the traits of zero and one, just as **Eleven** is treated positively as a double one or negatively as two, 1+1=2, the dark side of the Moon. **Twelve**, however, has a special place in the Bible because of the disciples and the tribes of Israel, both of which find parallels in the twelve signs of the zodiac. It represents strength in numbers, but those numbers are all intrinsic. **Thirteen** is the number of lunar months and can presage Moon qualities of the inner and after life, but with the possibility of regeneration. If thirteen features in a reading, it is a challenge to square up to a problem, be it business, health or a relationship, with honesty and resolution, and it will be overcome. The popular superstitions connected to this number rarely prevail.

# NUMBERS IN THE TAROT

In a Tarot reading, the numbers of the Major Arcana have special significance. This does not demean the Lesser Arcana, Staves, Cups, Swords and Pentacles, all of which have influence of a detailed nature which cannot be entered into in these pages.

Number One is **The Magician**, the channel of the life force and personal communication.

The horizontal eight, the symbol of infinity, is often incorporated as the brim of his hat. It represents achievement through attention to the final goal. Concentrate and you will succeed. Number Two, the **High Priestess**, is the feminine, subconscious mind. Fruitfulness of body or mind, harnessed to sensitive intuition, link her to the Magician. Think and then act. Number Three, the **Empress**, reveals feminine power, not in a physical or political sense, but related to the power of reproduction, growth and the fertility of ideas. Number Four is the **Emperor**, who rules the power of reason. He motivates and invigorates. He helps you get things done. Number Five, the **Pope** or **Hierophant**, suggests you listen more closely to your inner thoughts and gives you strength to rely on an intuitive understanding of factual analysis. Number Six, the **Two Lovers**, represents choice, not only in love, but at work or any other confrontational situation. Literally, smell is associated with six, but metaphorically it can indicate a nose which can smell out a correct solution. Once a choice is made it will probably be stuck to. Number Seven, the

**Chariot**, is the power of the mind to direct the body. The charioteer is never depicted holding the reins, his mind is in control. A sign of benevolent dominance, it can become perverted. Number Eight is a problematic number as it is often replaced by **Strength**, normally Number Eleven. Incarnated as **Justice** it reminds of the need to be logical and diplomatic. It also represents the need for balance in nature. Number Nine, the **Hermit**, lights the way and suggests taking time off to think and reassess. Meditation can be useful at difficult times.

Numerogically, nine ends the cycle. The composite numbers which follow keep some of the attributes of the single digits, added to by the digit they partner. Thus ten, (10) can become 1+0=1.

Number Ten is the seemingly cataclysmic **Wheel of Fortune**, but cycles of fortune do not consist of continuing disasters. For every down there is an up and the wheel gives the strength to overcome problems. Losing a job may be dramatic, but you may end up in a better one. Number Eleven

(1+1=2), **Strength**, signifies moral, psychical and physical strength through its number two connection to the Moon. Number Twelve (1+2=3) is the **Hanged Man**, really a mirror image as reflected in water. Things are not as they appear on the surface and a minor setback may be heralded. But the number three connection always suggests eventual expansion or growth. Number Thirteen (1+3=4) marks **Death**, not necessarily physical, but of ideas or ventures. Death also presages rebirth, so the number four connection of perseverance and work ethics suggests that you will

make it through the rain. Number Fourteen (1+4=5), **Temperance**, advises you to choose the middle path, particularly as number five warns of overindulgence of food, drink, drugs or sex. Number Fifteen (1+5=6), the **Devil**, suggests taking a positive line. Avoid the negative aspects of your personality and hope that the positive aspects of number six, a love of the arts and an honest attitude, come to your aid. Number Sixteen (1+6=7), the **Tower**, represents a flash of understanding, the proverbial bolt from the blue, which wakes you up and lets you see what is really happening. The number seven connection brings this intuition to a Tarot card which can often

be seen as negative. Number Seventeen (1+7=8), the **Star**, shows hope and revelation after the destruction of the Tower. Ideas will pour like water, as though reviving barren land. The infinite number eight does not impinge on this sign, other than to suggest continuity. Number Eighteen (1+8=9), the **Moon**, brings us to the end of the second cycle. The Moon is out again through the number nine influence, but the Mars connection invigorates. It is the sign of dreams and nightmares and shows the shadowy side of human nature. With number Nineteen (1=9=10, 1+0=1), the **Sun**, we return to number One. This is the card of

good fortune and health, made stronger by number One's leadership qualities. Number Twenty (2+0=2) is **Judgement**, revealing that all you achieve will be judged in this world and the next. You, too, can judge, but remember to judge as you would wish to be judged. The number Two, related to the instability of the Moon, can lead to indecisiveness and, therefore, bad judgement. Try to be balanced. Number Twenty-One (2+1=3), the **World**, is the last numbered card of the Tarot and represents completion and fulfilment. The four fixed signs of the zodiac on the card represent the basic laws of the universe which, if observed, lead to new beginnings. Number Three people are those who lead forward into the new cycle. The last card of the Major Arcana, **The Fool**, is not usually accorded a number, for he represents the primeval force, or nothingness, from which new life will appear.

## ACKNOWLEDGEMENTS

Illustrations are from the Waite Tarot Rider Pack, the Museo del Prado, Madrid, the Folks Museum, Holstebro, Denmark, the Kunsthistorisches Museum, Vienna, the Bibliotheque National (Giraudon) Paris, the Corcoran Collection, London, Grapharchive, London, and the Monte Carlo Casino, Monaco.

The publishers have made every effort to identify all illustration sources. Any errors and omissions will be corrected in future editions.